THE COST OF DELAYING ACTION TO STEM CLIMATE CHANGE

July 2014

Embargoed for 6:00 AM on July 29th

Executive Summary

The signs of climate change are all around us. The average temperature in the United States during the past decade was 0.8° Celsius (1.5° Fahrenheit) warmer than the 1901-1960 average, and the last decade was the warmest on record both in the United States and globally. Global sea levels are currently rising at approximately 1.25 inches per decade, and the rate of increase appears to be accelerating. Climate change is having different impacts across regions within the United States. In the West, heat waves have become more frequent and more intense, while heavy downpours are increasing throughout the lower 48 States and Alaska, especially in the Midwest and Northeast.[1] The scientific consensus is that these changes, and many others, are largely consequences of anthropogenic emissions of greenhouse gases.[2]

The emission of greenhouse gases such as carbon dioxide (CO_2) harms others in a way that is not reflected in the price of carbon-based energy, that is, CO_2 emissions create a negative externality. Because the price of carbon-based energy does not reflect the full costs, or economic damages, of CO_2 emissions, market forces result in a level of CO_2 emissions that is too high. Because of this market failure, public policies are needed to reduce CO_2 emissions and thereby to limit the damage to economies and the natural world from further climate change.

There is a vigorous public debate over whether to act now to stem climate change or instead to delay implementing mitigation policies until a future date. This report examines the economic consequences of delaying implementing such policies and reaches two main conclusions, both of which point to the benefits of implementing mitigation policies now and to the net costs of delaying taking such actions.

First, although delaying action can reduce costs in the short run, on net, delaying action to limit the effects of climate change is costly. Because CO_2 accumulates in the atmosphere, delaying action increases CO_2 concentrations. Thus, if a policy delay leads to higher ultimate CO_2 concentrations, that delay produces persistent economic damages that arise from higher temperatures and higher CO_2 concentrations. Alternatively, if a delayed policy still aims to hit a given climate target, such as limiting CO_2 concentration to given level, then that delay means that the policy, when implemented, must be more stringent and thus more costly in subsequent years. In either case, delay is costly.

These costs will take the form of either greater damages from climate change or higher costs associated with implementing more rapid reductions in greenhouse gas emissions. In practice, delay could result in both types of costs. These costs can be large:

---

[1] For a fuller treatment of the current and projected consequences of climate change for U.S. regions and sectors, see the Third National Climate Assessment (United States Global Change Research Program (USGCRP) 2014).
[2] See for example the Summary for Policymakers in Working Group I contribution to the Intergovernmental Panel on Climate Change Fifth Assessment Report (IPCC WG I AR5 2013).

- Based on a leading aggregate damage estimate in the climate economics literature, a delay that results in warming of 3° Celsius above preindustrial levels, instead of 2°, could increase economic damages by approximately 0.9 percent of global output. To put this percentage in perspective, 0.9 percent of estimated 2014 U.S. Gross Domestic Product (GDP) is approximately $150 billion. The incremental cost of an additional degree of warming beyond 3° Celsius would be even greater. Moreover, these costs are not one-time, but are rather incurred year after year because of the permanent damage caused by increased climate change resulting from the delay.

- An analysis of research on the cost of delay for hitting a specified climate target (typically, a given concentration of greenhouse gases) suggests that net mitigation costs increase, on average, by approximately 40 percent for each decade of delay. These costs are higher for more aggressive climate goals: each year of delay means more CO_2 emissions, so it becomes increasingly difficult, or even infeasible, to hit a climate target that is likely to yield only moderate temperature increases.

Second, climate policy can be thought of as "climate insurance" taken out against the most severe and irreversible potential consequences of climate change. Events such as the rapid melting of ice sheets and the consequent increase of global sea levels, or temperature increases on the higher end of the range of scientific uncertainty, could pose such severe economic consequences as reasonably to be thought of as climate catastrophes. Confronting the possibility of climate catastrophes means taking prudent steps now to reduce the future chances of the most severe consequences of climate change. The longer that action is postponed, the greater will be the concentration of CO_2 in the atmosphere and the greater is the risk. Just as businesses and individuals guard against severe financial risks by purchasing various forms of insurance, policymakers can take actions now that reduce the chances of triggering the most severe climate events. And, unlike conventional insurance policies, climate policy that serves as climate insurance is an investment that also leads to cleaner air, energy security, and benefits that are difficult to monetize like biological diversity.

I.   Introduction

The changing climate and increasing atmospheric greenhouse gas (GHG) concentrations are projected to accelerate multiple threats, including more severe storms, droughts, and heat waves, further sea level rise, more frequent and severe storm surge damage, and acidification of the oceans (USGCRP 2014). Beyond the sorts of gradual changes we have already experienced, global warming raises additional threats of large-scale changes, either changes to the global climate system, such as the disappearance of late-summer Arctic sea ice and the melting of large glacial ice sheets, or ecosystem impacts of climate change, such as critical endangerment or extinction of a large number of species.

Emissions of GHGs such as carbon dioxide (CO_2) generate a cost that is borne by present and future generations, that is, by people other than those generating the emissions. These costs, or economic damages, include costs to health, costs from sea level rise, and damage from increasingly severe storms, droughts, and wildfires. These costs are not reflected in the price of those emissions. In economists' jargon, emitting CO_2 generates a negative externality and thus a market failure. Because the price of CO_2 emissions does not reflect its true costs, market forces alone are not able to solve the problem of climate change. As a result, without policy action, there will be more emissions and less investment in emissions-reducing technology than there would be if the price of emissions reflected their true costs.

This report examines the cost of delaying policy actions to stem climate change, and reaches two main conclusions. First, delaying action is costly. If a policy delay leads to higher ultimate CO_2 concentrations, then that delay produces persistent additional economic damages caused by higher temperatures, more acidic oceans, and other consequences of higher CO_2 concentrations. Moreover, if delay means that the policy, when implemented, must be more stringent to meet a given target, then it will be more costly.

Second, uncertainty about the most severe, irreversible consequences of climate change adds urgency to implementing climate policies *now* that reduce GHG emissions. In fact, climate policy can be seen as climate insurance taken out against the most damaging potential consequences of climate change—consequences so severe that these events are sometimes referred to as climate catastrophes. The possibility of climate catastrophes leads to taking prudent steps now to sharply reduce the chances that they occur.

The costs of inaction underscore the importance of taking meaningful steps today towards reducing carbon emissions. An example of such a step is the Environmental Protection Agency's (EPA) proposed rule (2014) to regulate carbon pollution from existing power plants. By adopting economically efficient mechanisms to reduce emissions over the coming years, this proposed rule would generate large positive net benefits, which EPA estimates to be in the range of $27 - 50 billion annually in 2020 and $49 - 84 billion in 2030. These benefits include benefits to health from reducing particulate emissions as well as benefits from reducing CO_2 emissions.

Delaying Climate Policies Increases Costs

Delaying climate policies avoids or reduces expenditures on new pollution control technologies in the near term. But this short-term advantage must be set against the disadvantages, which are the costs of delay. The costs of delay are driven by fundamental elements of climate science and economics. Because the lifetime of CO_2 in the atmosphere is very long, if a mitigation policy is delayed, it must take as its starting point a higher atmospheric concentration of CO_2. As a result, delayed mitigation can result in two types of cost, which we would experience in different proportions depending on subsequent policy choices.

First, if delay means an increase in the ultimate end-point concentration of CO_2, then delay will result in additional warming and additional economic damages resulting from climate change. As is discussed in Section II, economists who have studied the costs of climate change find that temperature increases of 2° Celsius above preindustrial levels or less are likely to result in aggregate economic damages that are a small fraction of GDP. This small net effect masks important differences in which some regions could benefit somewhat from this warming while other regions could experience net costs. But global temperatures have *already* risen nearly 1° above preindustrial levels, and it will require concerted effort to hold temperature increases to within the narrow range consistent with small costs.[3] For temperature increases of 3° Celsius or more above preindustrial levels, the aggregate economic damages from climate change are expected to increase sharply.

Delay that causes a climate target to be missed creates large estimated economic damages. For example, a calculation in Section II of this report, based on a leading climate model (the DICE model as reported in Nordhaus 2013), shows that if a delay causes the mean global temperature increase to stabilize at 3° Celsius above preindustrial levels, instead of 2°, that delay will induce annual additional damages of approximately 0.9 percent of global output, as shown in Figure 1.[4] To put this percentage in perspective, 0.9 percent of estimated 2014 U.S. GDP is approximately $150 billion.[5] The next degree increase, from 3° to 4°, would incur greater *additional* annual costs of approximately 1.2 percent of global output. These costs are not one-time: they are incurred year after year because of the permanent damage caused by additional climate change resulting from the delay.

---

[3] The Working Group III contribution to the Intergovernmental Panel on Climate Change (IPCC) Fifth Assessment Report (IPCC WG III AR5 2014) does not analyze scenarios producing temperatures in 2100 less than 1.5 Celsius above preindustrial, because this is considered so difficult to achieve.

[4] Nordhaus (2013) stresses that these estimates "are subject to large uncertainties…because of the difficulty of estimating impacts in areas such as the value of lost species and damage to ecosystems." (pp. 139-140).

[5] These percentages apply to gross world output and the application of them to U.S. GDP is illustrative.

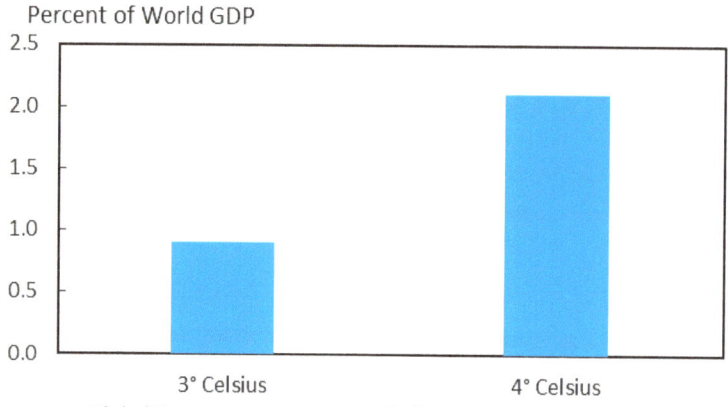

Figure 1: Economic Damage from Temperature Increase Beyond 2° Celsius

Source: Nordhaus (2013) and CEA calculations

The second type of cost of delay is the increased cost of reducing emissions more sharply if, instead, the delayed policy is to achieve the same climate target as the non-delayed policy. Taking meaningful steps now sends a signal to the market that reduces long-run costs of meeting the target. Part of this signal is that new carbon-intensive polluting facilities will be seen as bad investments; this reduces the amount of locked-in high-carbon infrastructure that is expensive to replace. Second, taking steps now to reduce CO_2 emissions signals the value of developing new low- and zero-emissions technologies, so additional steps towards a zero-carbon future can be taken as policy action incentivizes the development of new technologies. For both reasons, the least-cost mitigation path to achieve a given concentration target typically starts with a relatively low price of carbon to send these signals to the market, and subsequently increases as new low-carbon technology becomes available.[6]

The research discussed in Section II of this report shows that any short run gains from delay tend to be outweighed by the additional costs arising from the need to adopt a more abrupt and stringent policy later.[7] An analysis of the collective results from that research, described in more detail in Section II, suggests that the cost of hitting a specific climate target increases, on average, by approximately 40 percent for each decade of delay. These costs are higher for more aggressive climate goals: the longer the delay, the more difficult it becomes to hit a climate target. Furthermore, the research also finds that delay substantially decreases the chances that even concerted efforts in the future will hit the most aggressive climate targets.

---

[6] The 2010 National Research Council, *Limiting the Magnitude of Future Climate Change*, also stressed the importance of acting now to implement mitigation policies as a way to reduce costs. The NRC emphasized the importance of technology development in holding down costs, including by providing clear signals to the private sector through predictable policies that support development of and investment in low-carbon technologies.

[7] The IPCC WG III AR5 (2014) includes an extensive discussion of mitigation, including sectoral detail, potential for technological progress, and the timing of mitigation policies.

Although global action is essential to meet climate targets, unilateral steps both encourage broader action and benefit the United States. Climate change is a global problem, and it will require strong international leadership to secure cooperation among both developed and developing countries to solve it. America must help forge a truly global solution to this global challenge by galvanizing international action to significantly reduce emissions. By taking credible steps toward mitigation, the United States will also reap the benefits of early action, such as investing in low-carbon infrastructure now that will reduce the costs of reaching climate targets in the future.

Climate Policy as Climate Insurance

Individuals and businesses routinely purchase insurance to guard against various forms of risk such as fire, theft, or other loss. This logic of self-protection also applies to climate change. Much is known about the basic science of climate change: there is a scientific consensus that, because of anthropogenic emissions of CO_2 and other GHGs, global temperatures are increasing, sea levels are rising, and the world's oceans are becoming more acidic. These and other climate changes are expected to be harmful, on balance, to the world's natural and economic systems. Nevertheless, uncertainty remains about the magnitude and timing of these and other aspects of climate change, even if we assume that future climate policies are known in advance. For example, the Working Group I contribution to the IPCC's Fifth Assessment Report (IPCC WG I AR5 2013) provides a likely range of 1.5° to 4.5° Celsius for the equilibrium climate sensitivity, which is the long-run increase in global mean surface temperature that is caused by a sustained doubling of atmospheric CO_2 concentrations. The upper end of that range would imply severe climate impacts under current emissions trajectories, and current scientific knowledge indicates that values in excess of this range are also possible.[8]

An additional, related source of climate uncertainty is the possibility of irreversible, large-scale changes that have wide-ranging and severe consequences. These are sometimes called abrupt changes because they could occur extremely rapidly as measured in geologic time, and are also sometimes called climate catastrophes. We are already witnessing one of these events—the rapid trend towards disappearance of late-summer Arctic sea ice. A recent study from the National Research Council (NRC 2013) found that this strong trend toward decreasing sea-ice cover could have large effects on a variety of components of the Arctic ecosystem and could potentially alter large-scale atmospheric circulation and its variability. The NRC also found that another large-scale change has been occurring, which is the critical endangerment or loss of a significant percentage of marine and terrestrial species. Other events judged by the NRC to be likely in the more distant future (after 2100) include, for example, the possible rapid melting of the Western Antarctic ice and Greenland ice sheets and the potential thawing of Arctic permafrost and the consequent release of the potent GHG methane, which would accelerate global warming. These and other potential large-scale changes are irreversible on relevant time

---

[8] It is important to note that, as a global average, the equilibrium climate sensitivity masks the expectation that temperature change will be higher over land than the oceans, and that there will be substantial regional variations in temperature increases. The equilibrium climate sensitivity describes a long-term effect and is only one component of determining near term warming due to the buildup of GHGs in the atmosphere.

scales—if an ice sheet melts, it cannot be reconstituted—and they could potentially have massive global consequences and costs. For many of these events, there is thought to be a "tipping point," for example a temperature threshold, beyond which the transition to the new state becomes inevitable, but the values or locations of these tipping points are typically unknown.

Section III of this report examines the implications of these possible climate-related catastrophes for climate policy. Research on the economic and policy implications of such threats is relatively recent. As detailed in Section III, a conclusion that clearly emerges from this young but active literature is that the threat of a climate catastrophe, potentially triggered by crossing an unknown tipping point, implies erring on the side of prudence today. Accordingly, in a phrase used by Weitzman (2009, 2012), Pindyck (2011), and others, climate policy can be thought of as "climate insurance." The logic here is that of risk management, in which one acts now to reduce the chances of worst-case outcomes in the future. Here, too, there is a cost to delay: the longer emission reductions are postponed, the greater are atmospheric concentrations of GHGs, and the greater is the risk arising from delay.

Other Costs of Delay and Benefits of Acting Now

An additional benefit of adopting meaningful mitigation policies now is that doing so sends a strong signal to the market to spur the investments that will reduce mitigation costs in the future. An argument sometimes made is that mitigation policies should be postponed until new low-carbon technologies become available. Indeed, ongoing technological progress has dramatically improved productivity and welfare in the United States because of vast inventions and process improvements in the private sector (see for example CEA 2014, Chapter 6). The private sector invests in research and development, and especially in process improvements, because those technological advances reap private rewards. But low-carbon technologies, and environmental technologies more generally, face a unique barrier: their benefits – the reduction in global impacts of climate change – accrue to everyone and not just to the developer or adopter of such technologies.[9] Thus private sector investment in low-carbon technologies requires confidence that those investments, if successful, will pay off, that is, the private sector needs to have confidence that there will be a market for low-carbon technologies now and in the future. Public policies that set out a clear and ongoing mitigation path provide that confidence. Simply waiting for a technological solution, but not providing any reason for the private sector to create that solution, is not an effective policy. Although public financing of basic research is warranted because many of the benefits of basic research cannot be privately appropriated, many of the productivity improvements and cost reductions seen in new technologies come from incremental advances and process improvements that only arise through private-sector experience producing the product and learning-by-doing. These advances are protected through the patent system and as trade secrets, but those advances will only transpire if it is clear that they will have current and

---

[9] Popp, Newell, and Jaffe (2010) provide a thorough review of the literature regarding technological change and the environment.

future value. In other words, policy action induces technological change.[10] Although a full treatment of the literature on technological change is beyond the scope of this report, providing the private sector with the certainty needed to invest in low-carbon technologies and produce such technological change is a benefit of adopting meaningful mitigation policies now.

Finally, because this report examines the economic costs of delay, it focuses on actions or consequences that have a market price. But the total costs of climate change include much that does not trade in the market and to which it is difficult to assign a monetary value, such as the loss of habitat preservation, decreased value of ecosystem goods and services, and mass extinctions. Although some studies have attempted to quantify these costs, including all relevant climate impacts is infeasible. Accordingly, the monetized economic costs of delay analyzed in this report understate the true total cost of delaying action to mitigate climate change.

---

[10] For example, Popp (2003) provides empirical evidence that Title IV of the 1990 Clean Air Act Amendments (CAAA) led to innovations that reduced the cost of the environmental technologies that reduced SO_2 emissions from coal-fired power plants. Other literature shows evidence linking environmental regulation more broadly to innovation (e.g., Popp 2006, Jaffe and Palmer 1997, Lanjouw and Mody 1996).

II.   Costs from Delaying Policy Action

Delaying action on climate change can increase economic costs in two ways. First, if the delayed policy is no more stringent, it will miss the climate target of the original, non-delayed policy, resulting in atmospheric GHG concentrations that are permanently higher, thereby increasing the economic damages from climate change. Second, suppose a delayed policy alternatively strove to achieve the original climate target; if so, it would require a more stringent path to achieve that target. But this delayed, more stringent policy typically will result in additional mitigation costs by requiring more rapid adjustment later. In reality, delay might result in a mix of these two types of costs. The estimates of the costs of delay in this section draw on large bodies of research on these two types of costs. We first examine the economic damages from higher temperatures, then turn to the increased mitigation costs arising from delay.

Our focus here is on targets that limit GHG concentrations, both because this is what most of the "delay" literature considers and because concentration limits have been the focus of other assessments. These concentration targets are typically expressed as concentrations of CO_2-equivalent (CO_2e) GHGs, so they incorporate not just CO_2 concentrations but also methane and other GHGs. The CO_2e targets translate roughly into ranges of temperature changes as estimated by climate models and into the cumulative GHG emissions budgets discussed in some other climate literature. More stringent concentration targets decrease the odds that global average temperature exceeds 2°C above preindustrial levels by 2100. According to the IPCC WG III AR5 (2014), meeting a concentration target of 450 parts per million (ppm) CO_2e makes it "likely" (probability between 66 and 100 percent) that the temperature increase will be at most 2°C, relative to preindustrial levels, whereas stabilizing at a concentration level of 550 ppm CO_2e makes it "more unlikely than likely" (less than a 50 percent probability) that the temperature increase by 2100 will be limited to 2°C (IPCC WG III AR5 2014).[11]

Increasing Damages if Delay Means Missing Climate Targets

If delay means that a climate target slips, then the ultimate GHG concentrations, temperatures, and other changes in global climate would be greater than without the delay.[12]

A growing body of work examines the costs that climate change imposes on specific aspects of economic activity. The IPCC WG II AR5 (2014) surveys this growing literature and summarizes the impacts of projected climate change by sector. Impacts include decreased agricultural production; coastal flooding, erosion, and submergence; increases in heat-related illness and other stresses due to extreme weather events; reduction in water availability and quality;

---

[11] IPCC WG III AR5 (2014, ch. 6) provides a further refinement of these probabilities, associating a concentration target of 450 ppm of CO_2e with an approximate 70-85 percent probability of maintaining temperature change below 2°C, and a concentration level of 550 CO_2e with an approximate 30-45 percent probability of maintaining temperature change below 2°C.

[12] For information on the impacts of climate change at various levels of warming see *Climate Stabilization Targets: Emissions, Concentrations, and Impacts over Decades to Millennia* (NRC 2011).

displacement of people and increased risk of violent conflict; and species extinction and biodiversity loss. Although these impacts vary by region, and some impacts are not well-understood, evidence of these impacts has grown in recent years.[13]

A new class of empirical studies draw similar conclusions. Dell, Jones, and Olken (2013) review academic research that draws on historical variation in weather patterns to infer the effects of climate change on productivity, health, crime, political instability, and other social and economic outcomes. This approach complements physical science research by estimating the economic impacts of historical weather events that can be used to extrapolate to those expected in the future climate. The research finds evidence of economically meaningful impacts of climate change on a variety of outcomes. For example, when the temperature is greater than 100° Fahrenheit in the United States, labor supply in outdoor industries declines up to one hour per day relative to temperatures in the 76°-80° Fahrenheit range (Graff Zivin and Neidell 2014). Also in the United States, each additional day of extreme heat (exceeding 90° Fahrenheit) relative to a moderate day (50° to 59° Fahrenheit) increases the annual age-adjusted mortality rate by roughly 0.11 percent (Deschênes and Greenstone 2011).

These studies provide insights into the response of specific sectors or aspects of the economy to climate change. But because they focus on specific aspects of climate change, use different data sources, and use a variety of outcome measures, they do not provide direct estimates of the aggregate, or total, cost of climate change. Because estimating the total cost of climate change requires specifying future baseline economic and population trajectories, efforts to estimate the total cost of climate change typically rely on integrated assessment models (IAMs). IAMs are a class of economic and climate models that incorporate both climate and economic dynamics so that the climate responds to anthropogenic emissions and economic activity responds to the climate. In addition to projecting future climate variables and other economic variables, the IAMs estimate the total economic damages (and, in some cases, benefits) of climate change which includes impacts on agriculture, health, ecosystems services, productivity, heating and cooling demand, sea level rise, and adaptation.

Overall costs of climate change are substantial, according to IAMs. Nordhaus (2013) estimates global costs that increase with the rise in global average temperature, and Tol (2009, 2014) surveys various estimates. Two themes are common among these damage estimates. First, damage estimates remain uncertain, especially for large temperature increases. Second, the costs of climate change increase nonlinearly with the temperature change. Based on Nordhaus's (2013, Figure 22) net damage estimates, a 3° Celsius temperature increase above preindustrial levels, instead of 2°, results in additional damages of 0.9 percent of global output.[14] To put this

---

[13] The EPA's Climate Change Impacts and Risk Analysis project collects new research that estimates the potential damages of inaction and the benefits of GHG mitigation at national and regional scales for many important sectors, including human health, infrastructure, water resources, electricity demand and supply, ecosystems, agriculture, and forestry (Waldhoff et al. 2014).

[14] Some studies estimate that small temperature increases have a net economic *benefit*, for instance due to increased agricultural production in regions with colder climates. However, projected temperature increases even

percentage in perspective, 0.9 percent of estimated 2014 U.S. GDP is approximately $150 billion. The next degree increase, from 3° to 4°, would incur additional costs of 1.2 percent of global output. Moreover, these costs are not one-time, rather they recur year after year because of the permanent damage caused by increased climate change resulting from the delay. It should be stressed that these illustrative estimates are based on a single (albeit leading) model, and there is uncertainty associated with the aggregate monetized damage estimates from climate change; see for example the discussion in IPCC WG II AR5 (2014).

Increased Mitigation Costs from Delay

The second type of cost of delay arises if policy is delayed but still hits the climate target, for example stabilizing CO_2e concentrations at 550 ppm. Because a delay results in additional near-term accumulation of GHGs in the atmosphere, delay means that the policy, when implemented, must be more stringent to achieve the given long-term climate target. This additional stringency increases mitigation costs, relative to those that would be incurred under the least-cost path starting today.

This section reviews the recent literature on the additional mitigation costs of delay, under the assumption that both the original and delayed policy achieve a given climate target. We review 16 studies that compare 106 pairs of policy simulations based on integrated climate mitigation models (the studies are listed and briefly described in the Appendix). The simulations comprising each pair implement similar policies that lead to the same climate target (typically a concentration target but in some cases a temperature target) but differ in the timing of the policy implementation, nuanced in some cases by variation in when different countries adopt the policy. Because the climate target is the same for each scenario in the pair, the environmental and economic damages from climate change are approximately the same for each scenario. The additional cost of delaying implementation thus equals the difference in the mitigation costs in the two scenarios in each paired comparison. The studies reflect a broad array of climate targets, delayed timing scenarios, and modeling assumptions as discussed below. We focus on studies published in 2007 or later, including recent unpublished manuscripts.

In each case, a model computes the path of cost-effective mitigation policies, mitigation costs, and climate outcomes over time, constraining the emissions path so that the climate target is hit. Each path weighs technological progress in mitigation technology and other factors that encourage starting out slowly against the costs that arise if mitigation, delayed too long, must be undertaken rapidly. Because the models typically compute the policy in terms of a carbon price, the carbon price path computed by the model starts out relatively low and increases over the course of the policy. Thus a policy started today typically has a steadily increasing carbon price, whereas a delayed policy typically has a carbon price of zero until the start date, at which point it jumps to a higher initial level then increases more rapidly than the optimal immediate policy.

---

under immediate action fall in a range with a strong consensus that the costs of climate change exceed such benefits. The cost estimates presented here are net of any benefits expected to accrue.

The higher carbon prices after a delay typically lead to higher total costs than a policy that would impose the carbon price today.[15]

The IPCC WG III AR5 (2014) includes an overview of the literature on the cost of delayed action on climate change. They cite simulation studies showing that delay is costly, both when all countries delay action and when there is partial delay, with some countries delaying acting alone until there is a more coordinated international effort. The present report expands on that overview by further analyzing the findings of the studies considered by the IPCC report as well as additional studies. Like the IPCC report, we find broad agreement across the scenario pairs examined that delayed policy action is more costly compared to immediate action conditional on a particular climate target. This finding is consistent across a range of climate targets, policy participants, and modeling assumptions. The vast majority of studies estimate that delayed action incurs greater mitigation costs compared to immediate action. Furthermore, some models used in the research predict that the most stringent climate targets are feasible only if immediate action is taken under full participation. One implication is that considering only comparisons with numerical cost estimates may understate the true costs of delay, as failing to reach a climate target means incurring the costs from the associated climate change.

The costs of delay in these studies depend on a number of factors, including the length of delay, the climate target, modeling assumptions, future baseline emissions, future mitigation technology, delay scenarios, the participants implementing the policy, and geographic location. More aggressive targets are more costly to achieve, and meeting them is predicted to be particularly costly, if not infeasible, if action is delayed. Similarly, international coordination in policy action reduces mitigation costs, and the cost of delay depends on which countries participate in the policy, as well as the length of delay.

---

[15] Some models explicitly identify the carbon price path that minimizes total social costs. These optimization models always find equal or greater costs for scenarios with a delay constraint. Other models forecast carbon prices that result in the climate target but do not demand that the path results in minimal cost. These latter models can predict that delay reduces costs, and a small number of comparisons we review report negative delay costs.

THE ROLE OF TECHNOLOGICAL PROGRESS IN COST ESTIMATES

Assumptions about energy technology play an important role in estimating mitigation costs. For example, many models assume that carbon capture and storage (CCS) will enable point sources of emission to capture the bulk of carbon emissions and store them with minimal leakage into the atmosphere over a long period. Some comparisons also assume that CCS will combine with large-scale bio-energy ("bio-CCS"), effectively generating "negative emissions" since biological fuels extract atmospheric carbon during growth. Such technology could facilitate reaching a long-term atmospheric concentration target despite relatively modest near-term mitigation efforts. However, the IPCC warns that "There is only limited evidence on the potential for large-scale deployment of [bio-CCS], large-scale afforestation, and other [CO_2 removal] technologies and methods" (IPCC WG III AR5 2014). In addition, models must also specify the cost and timing of availability of such technology, potentially creating further variation in mitigation cost estimates.

The potential importance of technology, especially bio-CCS, is manifested in differences across models. Clarke et al. (2009) present delay cost estimates for 10 models simulating a 550 ppm CO_2 equivalent target by 2100 allowing for overshoot. The three models that assume bio-CCS availability estimate global present values of the cost of delay ranging from $1.4 trillion to $4.7 trillion. Among the seven models without bio-CCS, four predict higher delay costs, one predicts that the concentration target was infeasible under a delay, and two predict lower delay costs. The importance of bio-CCS is even clearer with a more stringent target. For example, two of the three models with bio-CCS find that a 450 ppm CO_2 equivalent target is feasible under a delay scenario, while none of the seven models without bio-CCS find the stringent target to be feasible.

The Department of Energy sponsors ongoing research on CCS for coal-fired power plants. As part of its nearly $6 billion commitment to clean coal technology, the Administration, partnered with industry, has already invested in four commercial-scale and 24 industrial-scale CCS projects that together will store more than 15 million metric tons of CO_2 per year.

An important determinant of costs is the role of technological progress and the availability of mitigation technologies (see the box). The models typically assume technological progress in mitigation technology, which means that the cost of reducing emissions declines over time as energy technologies improve. As a result, it is cost-effective to start with a relatively less stringent policy, then increase stringency over time, and the models typically build in this cost-effective tradeoff. However, most models still find that immediate initiation of a less stringent policy followed by increasing stringency incurs lower costs than delaying policy entirely and then increasing stringency more rapidly.

We begin by characterizing the primary findings in the literature broadly, discussing the estimates of delay costs and how the costs vary based on key parameters of the policy scenarios; additional details can be found in the Appendix. We then turn to a statistical analysis of all the available delay cost estimates that we could gather in a standardized form, that is, we conduct a meta-analysis of the literature on delay cost estimates.

Effect on Costs of Climate Targets, Length of Delay, and International Coordination

Climate Targets

Researchers estimate a range of climate and economic impacts from a given concentration of GHGs and find that delaying action is much costlier for more stringent targets. Two recent major modeling simulation projects conducted by the Energy Modeling Forum (Clarke et al. 2009) and by AMPERE (Riahi et al. 2014) consider the economic costs of delaying policies to reach a range of CO_2e concentration targets from 450 to 650 ppm in 2100. In the Energy Modeling Forum simulations in Clarke et al. (2009), the median additional cost (global present value) for a 20-year delay is estimated to be $0.7 trillion for 650 ppm CO_2e but a substantially greater $4.7 trillion for 550 ppm CO_2e. Many of the models in these studies suggest that delay causes a target of 450 ppm CO_2e to be much more costly to achieve, or possibly even infeasible.

Length of Delay

The longer the delay, the greater the cumulative emissions before action begins and the shorter the available time to meet a given target. Several recent studies examine the cost implications of delayed climate action and find that even a short delay can add substantial costs to meeting a stringent concentration target, or even make the target impossible to meet. For example, Luderer et al. (2012) find that delay from 2010 to 2020 to stabilize CO_2 concentration levels at 450 ppm by 2100 raises mitigation cost by 50 to 700 percent.[16] Furthermore, Luderer et al. find that delay until 2030 renders the 450 ppm target infeasible. Edmonds et al. (2008) find that additional mitigation costs of delay by newly developed and developing countries are substantial. In fact, they find that stabilizing CO_2 concentrations at 450 ppm even for a relatively short delay from 2012 to 2020 increases costs by 28 percent over the idealized case, and a delay to 2035 increased costs by more than 250 percent.

International Coordination

Meeting stringent climate targets with action from only one country or a small group of countries is difficult or impossible, making international coordination of policies essential. Recent research shows, however, that even if a delay in international mitigation efforts occurs, unilateral or fragmented action reduces the costs of delay: although immediate coordinated international action is the least costly approach, unilateral action is less costly than doing nothing.[17] More specifically, Jakob et al. (2012) consider a 10-year delay of mitigation efforts to reach a 450 ppm CO_2 target by 2100 and find that global mitigation costs increase by 43 to 700 percent if all countries begin mitigation efforts in 2020 rather than 2010. However, early action in 2010 by more developed countries reduces this increase to 29 to 300 percent. In a similar scenario,

---

[16] We present a range of cost estimates which comes from the three IAMs – ReMIND-R, WITCH and IMACLIM-R – used by Luderer et al. (2012). These scenarios also allow temporary overshoot of the target.

[17] Waldhoff and Fawcett (2011) find that early mitigation action by industrialized economies significantly reduces the likelihood of large temperature changes in 2100 while also increasing the likelihood of lower temperature changes, relative to a no policy scenario.

Luderer et al. (2012) find that costs increase by 50 to 700 percent with global delay from 2010 to 2020, however if the industrialized countries begin mitigation efforts unilaterally in 2010 (and are joined by all countries in 2020), the estimated cost increases range from zero to about 200 percent. Luderer et al. (2013) and Riahi et al. (2014) find that costs of delay are smaller when fewer countries delay mitigation efforts, or when short-term actions during the delay are more aggressive.

Jakob et al. (2012) find it is in the best interest of the European Union to begin climate action in 2010 rather than delaying action with all other countries until 2020. They also estimate that the cost increase to the United States from delaying climate action with all other countries until 2020 is from 28 to 225 percent, relative to acting early along with other industrialized economies.[18] McKibbin, Morris, and Wilcoxen (2014) consider the impact that a delay in imposing a unilateral price of carbon would have on economic outcomes in the United States including GDP, investment, consumption and employment. They find that although unilateral mitigation efforts do incur costs, delay is costlier.

Summary: Quantifying Patterns across the Studies

We now turn to a quantitative summary and assessment, or meta-analysis, of the studies discussed above.[19] The data set for this analysis consists of the results on all available numerical estimates of the average or total cost of delayed action from our literature search. Each estimate is a paired comparison of a delay scenario and its companion scenario without delay. To make results comparable across studies, we convert the delay cost estimates (presented in the original studies variously as present values of dollars, percent of consumption, or percent of GDP) to percent change in costs as a result of delay.[20] We capture variation across study and experimental designs using variables that encode the length of the delay in years; the target CO_2e concentration; whether only the relatively more-developed countries act immediately (partial delay); the discount rate used to calculate costs; and the model used for the simulation.[21] All comparisons consider policies and outcomes measured approximately through the end of the century. To reduce the effect of outliers, the primary regression analysis only uses results with less than a 400 percent increase in costs (alternative methods of handling the outliers are

---

[18] Note that the IMACLIM model finds that U.S. mitigation declines to the point in which they are slightly negative (i.e. net gains compared to business-as-usual).

[19] A study of the results of other studies is referred to as a meta-analysis, and there is a rich body of statistical tools for meta-analysis, see for example Borenstein et al. (2009).

[20] For example, if in some paired comparison delay increased mitigation costs from 0.20 percent of GDP to 0.30 percent of GDP, the cost increase would be 50 percent. Comparisons for which the studies provided insufficient information to calculate the percentage increase in costs (including all comparisons from Riahi et al. 2014) are excluded. Also excluded are comparisons that report only the market price of carbon emissions at the end of the simulation, which is not necessarily proportional to total mitigation costs.

[21] When measuring delay length for policies with multiple stages of implementation, we count the delay as ending at the start of any new participation in mitigation by any party after the start of the simulation. We also exclude scenarios with delays exceeding 30 years. When other climate targets were provided (e.g., CO_2 concentration or global average temperature increase), the corresponding CO_2e concentration levels are estimated using conversions from IPCC WG III AR5 (2014).

discussed below as sensitivity checks), and only includes paired comparisons for which both the primary and delayed policies are feasible (i.e. the model was able to solve for both cases).[22] The dataset contains a total of 106 observations (paired comparisons), with 58 included in the primary analysis. All observations in the data set are weighted equally.

Analysis of these data suggests two main conclusions, both consistent with findings from specific papers in the underlying literature. The first is that, looking across studies, costs increase with the length of the delay. Figure 2 shows the delay costs as a function of the delay time. Although there is considerable variability in costs for a given delay length because of variations across models and experiments, there is an overall pattern of costs increasing with delay.

Figure 2: Additional Mitigation Costs of Delay by Length

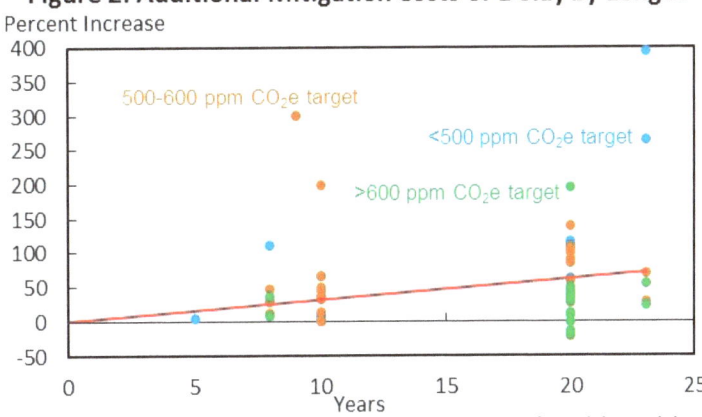

Notes: Data points are percentage increase in mitigation costs from delay and the associated length of delay for a given paired simulation. The scatterplot presents a total of 58 paired delay simulations. The solid line is the regression fit to these data, restricted to pass through the origin.
Source: CEA calculations.

For example, of the 14 paired simulations with 10 years of delay (these are represented by the points in Figure 2 with 10 years of delay), the average delay cost is 39 percent. The regression line shown in Figure 2 estimates an average cost of delay per year using all 58 paired experiments under the assumption of a constant increasing delay cost per year (and, by definition, no cost if there is no delay), and this estimate is 37 percent per decade. This analysis ignores possible confounding factors, such as longer delays being associated with less stringent targets, and the multiple regression analysis presented below controls for such confounding factors.

The second conclusion is that the more ambitious the climate target, the greater are the costs of delay. This can be seen in Figure 3, in which the lowest (most stringent) concentration targets tend to have the highest cost estimates. In fact, close inspection of Figure 2 reveals a related pattern: the relationship between delay length and additional costs is steeper for the points representing CO_2e targets of 500 ppm or less than for those in the other two ranges. That is, costs

---

[22] In the event that a model estimates a cost for a first-best scenario but determines the corresponding delay scenario to be infeasible, the comparison is coded as having costs exceeding 400 percent. In addition, one comparison from Clarke et al. (2009) is excluded because a negative baseline cost precludes the calculation of a percent increase.

of delay are particularly high for scenarios with the most stringent target and the longest delay lengths.

Figure 3: Additional Mitigation Costs by CO₂ Concentration

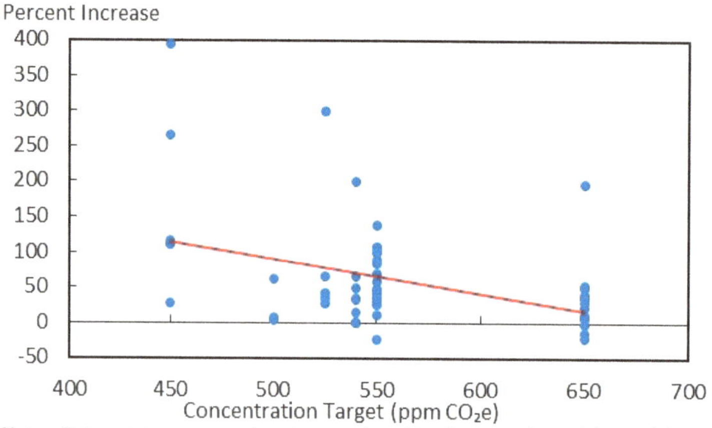

Notes: Data points are percentage increase in mitigation costs from delay and the associated CO₂ concetration target for a given paired simulation. The scatterplot presents a total of 58 paired delay simulations. The solid line is the regression line fit to these data.

Table 1 presents the results of multiple regression analysis that summarizes how various factors affect predictions from the included studies, holding constant the other variables included in the regression. The dependent variable is the cost of delay, measured as the percentage increase relative to the comparable no-delay scenario, and the length of delay is measured in decades. Specifications (1) and (2) correspond to Figures 2 and 3, respectively. Each subsequent specification includes the length of the delay in years, an indicator variable for a partial delay scenario, and the target CO₂e concentration. In addition to the coefficients shown, specification (4) includes model fixed effects, which control for systematic differences across models, and each specification other than column (1) includes an intercept.

The results in Table 1 quantify the two main findings mentioned above. The coefficients in column (3) indicate that, looking across these studies, a one decade increase in delay length is on average associated with a 41 percent increase in mitigation cost relative to the no-delay scenario. This regression does not control for possible differences in baseline costs across the different models, however, so column (4) reports a variant that includes an additional set of binary variables indicating the model used ("model fixed effects"). Including model fixed effects increases the delay cost to 56 percent per decade. When the cost of a delay is estimated separately for different concentration target bins (column (5)), delay is more costly the more ambitious is the concentration target. But even for the least ambitious target – a CO₂e concentration exceeding 600 ppm – delay is estimated to increase costs by approximately 24 percent per decade. Because of the relatively small number of cases (58 paired comparisons), which are further reduced when delay is estimated within target bins, the standard errors are large, especially for the least ambitious scenarios, so for an overall estimate of the delay cost we do not differentiate between the different targets. While the regression in column (4) desirably controls for differences across models, other (unreported) specifications that handle the outliers in different ways and include other control variables give per-decade delay estimates both larger and smaller than the regression in column (3).[23] We therefore adopt the estimate in regression (3) of 41 percent per decade as the overall annual estimate of delay costs.

One caveat concerning this analysis is that it only considers cases in which model solutions exist. The omitted, infeasible cases tend to be ones with ambitious targets that cannot be met when there is long delay, given the model's technology assumptions. For this reason, omitting these cases arguably understates the costs of delay reported in Table 1.[24] Additionally, we note that estimates of the effect of a partial delay (when some developed nations act now and other nations delay action) are imprecisely estimated, perhaps reflecting the heterogeneity of partial delay scenarios examined in the studies.

---

[23] The results in Table 1 are generally robust to using a variety of other specifications and regression methods, including: using the percent decrease from the delay case, instead of the percent increase from the no-delay case, as the dependent variable as an alternative way to handle outliers; using median regression, also as an alternative way to handle outliers; and including the discount factor as additional explanation of variation in the cost of delay, but this coefficient is never statistically significant. These regressions use linear compounding, not exponential, because the focus is on the per-decade delay cost not the annual delay cost. An alternative approach is to specify the dependent variable in logarithms (although this eliminates the negative estimates), and doing so yields generally similar results after compounding to those in Table 1.

[24] An alternative approach to omitting the infeasible-solution observations is to treat their values as censored at some level. Accordingly, the regressions in Table 1 were re-estimated using tobit regression, for which values exceeding 400 percent (including the non-solution cases) are treated as censored. As expected, the estimated costs of delay per year estimated by tobit regression exceed the ordinary least squares estimates. A linear probability model (not shown) indicates that scenarios with longer delay and more stringent targets are more likely to have delay cost increases exceeding 400 percent (including non-solution cases). The assumption of bio-CCS technology has no statistically significant correlation with delay cost increase in a censored regression but is associated with a significantly lower probability of delay cost increases exceeding 400 percent.

Table 1: Increased Mitigation Costs Resulting from a Delay, Given a Specified Climate Target: Regression Results

	(1)	(2)	(3)	(4)	(5)
Delay (decades)	37.3***		41.1**	56.3***	
	(5.9)		(17.0)	(18.2)	
Delay (decades) x ppm $CO_2e \leq 500$					66.7**
					(27.1)
Delay (decades) x $500 < ppm\ CO_2e \leq 600$					24.9
					(18.5)
Delay (decades) x ppm $CO_2e > 600$					24.1
					(33.9)
Partial delay			8.3	-20.0	14.8
			(26.0)	(27.8)	(25.7)
Target CO_2e concentration		-0.49***	-0.61***	-0.61***	-0.30
		(0.16)	(0.16)	(0.15)	(0.49)
Model fixed effects?	No	No	No	Yes	No
Observations	58	58	58	58	58
R-squared	0.41	0.15	0.24	0.53	0.30

Notes: The table presents ordinary least squares regression coefficients, with each column representing a different regression. For each, the dependent variable is the percent increase in cost from a scenario involving no delay to a scenario involving a delay. Each observation is a comparison of a pair of scenarios with the same climate target, for a total of 58 observations. The regressors represent some of the variables that characterize each paired comparison: the simulated delay, the delay interacted with the concentration target (binned), whether only some countries delayed (partial delay), and the target concentration. The appendix lists all studies from which the data were drawn. The specification in column (1) does not include a constant.

Significant at the: *10% **5% ***1% significance level.

Source: CEA calculations on results from studies listed in appendix.

III. Climate Policy as Climate Insurance

As discussed in the 2013 NRC report, *Abrupt Impacts of Climate Change: Anticipating Surprises*, the Earth's climate history suggests the existence of "tipping points," that is, thresholds beyond which major changes occur that may be self-reinforcing and are likely to be irreversible over relevant time scales. Some of these changes, such as the rapid decline in late-summer Arctic sea ice, are already under way. Others represent potential events for which a tipping point likely exists, but cannot at the present be located. For example, there is new evidence that we might already have crossed a previously unrecognized tipping point concerning the destabilization of the West Antarctic Ice Sheet (Joughin, Smith, and Medley 2014 and Rignot et. al. 2014). A tipping point that is unknown, but thought unlikely to be reached in this century, is the release of methane from thawing Arctic permafrost, which could reinforce the greenhouse effect and spur additional warming and exacerbate climate change. Tipping points can also be crossed by slower climate changes that exceed a threshold at which there is a large-scale change in a biological system, such as the rapid extinction of species. Such impacts could pose such severe consequences for societies and economies that they are sometimes called potential climate catastrophes.

This section examines the implications of these potentially severe outcomes for climate policy, a topic that has been the focus of considerable recent research in the economics literature. The main conclusion emerging from this growing body of work is that the potential of these events to have large-scale impacts has important implications for climate policy. Because the probability of a climate catastrophe increases as GHG emissions rise, missing climate targets because of postponed policies increases risks. Uncertainty about the likelihood and consequences of potential climate catastrophes adds further urgency to implementing policies now to reduce GHG emissions.

Tail Risk Uncertainty and Possible Large-Scale Changes

Were some of these large-scale events to occur, they would have severe consequences and would effectively be irreversible. Because these events are thought to be relatively unlikely, at least in the near term – that is, they occur in the "tail" of the distribution – but would have severe consequences, they are sometimes referred to as "tail risk" events. Because these tail risk events are outside the range of modern human experience, uncertainty surrounds both the science of their dynamics and the economics of their consequences.

Because many of these events are triggered by warming, their likelihood depends in part on the equilibrium climate sensitivity. The IPCC WG I AR5 (2013) provides a likely range of 1.5° to 4.5° Celsius for the equilibrium climate sensitivity. However, considerably larger values cannot be ruled out and are more likely than lower values (i.e. the probability distribution is skewed towards higher values). Combinations of high climate sensitivity and high GHG emissions can result in extremely large end-of-century temperature changes. For example, the IPCC WG III AR5 (2014) cites a high-end projected warming of 7.8° Celsius by 2100, relative to 1900-1950.

A second way to express this risk is to focus on specific large-scale changes in Earth or biological systems that could be triggered and locked in by GHG concentrations rising beyond a certain point. At higher climate sensitivities, the larger temperature response to atmospheric GHG concentrations would make it even more likely that we would cross temperature-related tipping points in the climate system. The potential for additional releases of methane, a potent GHG, from thawing permafrost, thus creating a positive feedback to further increase temperatures, is an example of such a tail risk event. Higher carbon dioxide concentrations in the atmosphere, by increasing the acidity of the oceans, could also trigger and lock in permanent changes to ocean ecosystems, such as diminished coral reef-building, which decreases biodiversity supported on reefs and decreases the breakwater effects that protect shorelines. The probability of significant negative effects from ocean acidification can be increased by other stressors such as higher temperatures and overfishing.

The box summarizes some of these potential large-scale events, which are sometimes also referred to as "abrupt" because they occur in a very brief period of geological time. These events are sufficiently large-scale they have the potential for severely disrupting ecosystems and human societies, and thus are sometimes referred to as catastrophic outcomes.

ABRUPT IMPACTS OF CLIMATE CHANGE: ANTICIPATING SURPRISES

The National Research Council's 2013 report, *Abrupt Impacts of Climate Change: Anticipating Surprises*, discusses a number of abrupt climate changes with potentially severe consequences. These events include:

- **Late-summer Arctic sea ice disappearance:** Strong trends of accelerating late-summer sea ice loss have been observed in the Arctic. The melting of Arctic sea ice comprises a positive feedback loop, as less ice means more sunlight will be absorbed into the dark ocean, causing further warming.
- **Sea level rise (SLR) from destabilization of West Antarctic ice sheets (WAIS):** The WAIS represents a potential SLR of 3-4 meters as well as coastal inundation and stronger storm surges. Much remains unknown of the physical processes at the ice-ocean frontier. However, two recent studies (Joughin, Smith, and Medley 2014, Rignot et. al. 2014) report evidence that irreversible WAIS destabilization has already started.
- **Sea level rise from other ice sheets melting:** Losing all other ice sheets, including Greenland, may cause SLR of up to 60 meters as well as coastal inundation and stronger storm surges. Melting of the Greenland ice sheet alone may induce SLR of 7m, but it is not expected to destabilize rapidly within this century.
- **Disruption to Atlantic Meridional Overturning Circulation (AMOC):** Potential disruptions to the AMOC may disrupt local marine ecosystems and shift tropical rain belts southward. Although current models do not indicate that an abrupt shift in the AMOC is likely within the century, the deep ocean remains understudied with respect to measures necessary for AMOC calculations.
- **Decrease in ocean oxygen:** As the solubility of gases decrease with rising temperature, a warming of the ocean will decrease the oxygen content in the surface ocean and expand existing Oxygen Minimum Zones. This will pose a threat to aerobic marine life as well as release nitrous oxide—a potent GHG—as a byproduct of microbial processes. The NRC study assesses a moderate likelihood of an abrupt increase in oxygen minimum zones in this century.
- **Increasing release of carbon stores in soils and permafrost:** Northern permafrost contains enough carbon to trigger a positive feedback response to warming temperatures. With an estimated stock of 1700-1800 Gt, the permafrost carbon stock could amplify considerably human-induced climate change. Small trends in soil carbon releases have been already observed.
- **Increasing release of methane from ocean methane hydrates:** This is a particularly potent long-term risk due to hydrate deposits through changes in ocean water temperature; the likely timescale for the physical processes involved spans centuries, however, and there is low risk this century.

- **Rapid state changes in ecosystems, species range shifts, and species boundary changes:** Research shows that climate change is an important component of abrupt ecosystem state-changes, with a prominent example being the Sahel region of Africa. Such state-changes from forests to savanna, from savanna to grassland, et cetera, will cause extensive habitat loss to animal species and threaten food and water supplies. The NRC study assesses moderate risk during this century and high risk afterwards.
- **Increases in extinctions of marine and terrestrial species:** Abrupt climate impacts include extensive extinctions of marine and terrestrial species; examples such as the destruction of coral reef ecosystems are already underway. Numerous land mammal, bird, and amphibian species are expected to become extinct with a high probability within the next one or two centuries.

Implications of Tail Risk

An implication of the theory of decision-making under uncertainty is that the risks posed by irreversible catastrophic events can be substantial enough to influence or even dominate decisions.

Weitzman's Dismal Theorem

Over the past few years, economists have examined the implications of decision-making under uncertainty for climate change policy. In a particularly influential treatment, Weitzman (2009) proposes his so-called "Dismal Theorem," which provides a set of assumptions under which the current generation would be willing to bear very large (in fact, arbitrarily large) costs to avoid a future event with widespread, large-scale costs. The intuition behind Weitzman's mathematical result rests with the basic insight that because individuals are risk-averse, they prefer to buy health, home, and auto insurance than to take their chances of a major financial loss. Similarly, if major climate events have the potential to reduce aggregate consumption by a large amount, society will be better off if it can take out "climate insurance" by paying mitigation costs now that will reduce the odds of a large-scale—in Weitzman's (2009) word, catastrophic—drop in consumption later.[25]

---

[25] This logic has its basis in expected utility theory. Because individuals are risk averse, each additional dollar of consumption provides less value, or utility, to individuals than the previous dollar. To avoid this major loss, an individual will buy home insurance. That insurance is provided by the market because an insurance company can offer home insurance to many homeowners in different regions of the country, and through diversification the company will on average have many homeowners paying premiums and a few collecting insurance, so diversification allows the company to run a relatively low-risk business. But risks from severe climate change are not diversifiable because their enormous costs would impact the global economy. Consequently, as long as there is a non-negligible probability of a large drop in consumption, and therefore a very large drop in utility, arising from a large-scale loss in consumption, society today should be willing to pay a substantial amount if doing so would avoid that loss.

Weitzman's (2009) dismal theorem has spurred a substantial amount of research on the economics of what this literature often refers to as climate catastrophes. A number of authors (e.g. Newbold and Daigneault 2009, Ackerman et al. 2010, Pindyck 2011, 2013, Nordhaus 2011, 2012, Litterman 2013, Millner 2013), including Weitzman (2011, 2014), stress that although the strong version of Weitzman's (2009) result—that society would be willing to pay an arbitrarily large amount to avoid future large-scale economic losses—depends on specific mathematical assumptions, the general principle of taking action to prevent such events does not. The basic insight is that, just as the sufficiently high threat of a fire justifies purchasing homeowners insurance, the threat of large-scale losses from climate change justifies purchasing "climate insurance" in the form of mitigation policies now (Pindyck 2011), and that taking actions today could help to avoid worst-case outcomes (Hwang, Tol, and Hofkes 2013). According to this line of thinking, the difficulty of assessing the probabilities of such large-scale losses or the location of tipping points does not change the basic conclusion that, because their potential costs are so overwhelming, the threat of very large losses due to climate change warrants implementing mitigation policies now.

Several recent studies have started down the road of quantifying the implications of the precautionary motive for climate policy. One approach is to build the effects of large-scale changes into IAMs, either by modeling the different risks explicitly or by simulation using heavy-tailed distributions for key parameters such as the equilibrium climate sensitivity or parameters of the economic damage function. Research along these lines includes Ackerman, Stanton, and Bueno (2013), Pycroft et al. (2011), Dietz (2011), Ceronsky et al. (2011), and Link and Tol (2011). Another approach is to focus on valuation of the extreme risks themselves outside an IAM, for example as examined by Pindyck (2012) and van der Ploeg and de Zeeuw (2013). Kopits, Marten, and Wolverton (2013) review some of the tail risk literature and literature on large-scale Earth system changes, and suggest steps forward for incorporating such events in IAMs, identifying ways in which the modeling could be improved even within current IAM frameworks and where additional work is needed. One of the challenges in assessing these large-scale events is that some of the most extreme events could occur in the distant future, and valuing consumption losses beyond this century raises additional uncertainty about intervening economic growth rates and questions about how to discount the distant future.[26] The literature is robust in showing that the potential for such events could have important climate policy implications, however, the scientific community has yet to derive robust quantitative policy recommendations based on a detailed analyses of the link between possible large-scale Earth system changes and their economic consequences.

Implications of Uncertainty about Tipping Points
Although research that embeds tipping points into climate models is young, one qualitative conclusion is that the prospect of a potential tipping point with unknown location enhances the precautionary motive for climate policy (Baranzini, Chesney, and Morisset 2003, Brozovic and Schlenker 2011, Cai, Judd, and Lontzek 2013, Lemoine and Traeger 2012, Barro 2013, van der

---

[26] For various perspectives on the challenges of evaluating long-term climate risks, see Dasgupta (2008), Barro (2013), Ackerman, Stanton, and Bueno (2013), Roe and Bauman (2013), and Weitzman (2013).

Ploeg 2014). To develop the intuition, first suppose that the tipping point is a known temperature increase, say 3° Celsius above preindustrial levels, and that the economic consequences of crossing the tipping point are severe, and temporarily put aside other reasons for reducing carbon emissions. Under these assumptions climate policy would allow temperature to rise, stopping just short of the 3° increase. In contrast, now suppose that the tipping point is unknown and that its estimated mean is 3°, but that it could be less or more with equal probability. In this case, the policy that stops just short of 3° warming runs a large risk of crossing the true tipping point. Because that mistake would be very costly, the uncertainty about the tipping point generally leads to a policy that is more stringent today than it would be absent uncertainty. To the extent that delayed implementation means higher long-run CO_2 concentrations, then the risks of hitting a tipping point increase with delay.

As a simplification, the above description assumes away other costs of climate change that increase smoothly with temperature, as well as the reality that important tipping points in biological systems could be crossed by small gradual changes in temperatures, so as to focus on the consequences of uncertainty about large-scale temperature changes. When the two sets of costs are combined, the presence of potential large-scale changes increases the benefits of mitigation policies, and the presence of uncertainty about tipping points that would produce abrupt changes increases those benefits further.[27] Cai, Judd, and Lontzek (2013) use a dynamic stochastic general equilibrium version of DICE model that is modified to include multiple tipping points with unknown (random) locations. To avoid the Weitzman "infinities" problem, they focus on tipping events with economic consequences that are large (5 or 10 percent of global GDP) but fall short of global economic collapses. They conclude that the possibility of future tipping points increases the optimal carbon price today: in their benchmark case, the optimal pre-tipping carbon price more than doubles, relative to having no tipping point dynamics. Similarly, Lemoine and Traeger (2012) embed unknown tipping points in the DICE model and estimate that the optimal carbon price increases by 45 percent as a result. In complementary work, Barro (2013) considers a simplified model in which the only benefits of reducing carbon emissions come from reducing the probability of potential climate catastrophes, and finds that this channel alone can justify investment in reducing GHG pollution of one percent of GDP or more, beyond what would normally occur in the market absent climate policy.

---

[27] Cai, Judd, and Lontzek (2013) provide a stark example of this dynamic. Their analysis, which is undertaken using a modified version of Nordhaus's (2008) DICE-2007 model, includes both the usual reasons for emissions mitigation (damages that increase smoothly with temperature) and the possibility of a tipping point at an uncertain future temperature which results in a jump in damages.

References

Ackerman, Frank, Stephen J. DeCanio, Richard B. Howarth, and Kristen Sheeran. 2010. "The Need for a Fresh Approach to Climate Change Economics." In *Assessing the Benefits of Avoided Climate Change: Cost-Benefit Analysis and Beyond*: 159-181.

Ackerman, Frank, Elizabeth A. Stanton, and Ramón Bueno. 2013. "Epstein-Zin Utility in DICE: Is Risk Aversion Irrelevant to Climate Policy?" *Environmental Resource Economics* 56, 1: 73-84.

Barranzani, Andrea, Marc Chesney, and Jacques Morisset. 2003. "The Impact of Possible Climate Catastrophes on Global Warming Policy." *Energy Policy* 31, 8: 691-701.

Barro, Robert J. 2013. "Environmental Protection, Rare Disasters, and Discount Rates." *NBER Working Paper* 19258.

Blanford, Geoffrey J., Richard G. Richels, and Thomas F. Rutherford. 2009. "Feasible Climate Targets: The Roles of Economic Growth, Coalition Development and Expectations." *Energy Economics* 31, supplement 2: S82-S93.

Borenstein, Michael, Larry V. Hedges, Julian P.T. Higgins, and Hannah Rothstein. 2009. *Introduction to Meta-Analysis*. Chichester, U.K.: Wiley.

Bosetti, Valentina, Carlo Carraro, and Massimo Tavoni. 2009. "Climate Change Mitigation Strategies in Fast-Growing Countries: the Benefits of Early Action." *Energy Economics* 31, supplement 2: S14-S151.

Bosetti, Valentina, Carlo Carraro, Alessandra Sgobbi, and Massimo Tavoni. 2009. "Delayed Action and Uncertain Stabilisation Targets. How Much Will the Delay Cost?" *Climatic Change* 96, 3: 299-312.

Brozovic, N. and W. Schlenker. 2011. "Optimal Management of an Ecosystem with an Unknown Threshold." *Ecological Economics* 70, 4: 627-640.

Cai, Yonyang, Kenneth L. Judd, and Thomas S. Lontzek. 2013. "The Social Cost of Stochastic and Irreversible Climate Change." *NBER Working Paper* 18704.

Calvin, Katherine, James Edmonds, Ben Bond-Lamberty, Leon Clarke, Son H. Kim, Page Kyle, Steven J. Smith, Allison Thomson, and Marshall Wise. 2009a. "Limiting Climate Change to 450 ppm CO_2 Equivalent in the 21st Century." *Energy Economics* 31, supplement 2: S107-S120.

Calvin, Katherine, Pralit Patel, Allen Fawcett, Leon Clarke, Karen Fisher-Vanden, Jae Edmonds, Son H. Kim, Ron Sands, and Marshall Wise. 2009b. "The Distribution and Magnitude of Emissions Mitigation Costs in Climate Stabilization under Less Than Perfect International Cooperation: SGM Results." *Energy Economics* 31, supplement 2: S187-S197.

Ceronsky, Megan, David Anthoff, Cameron Hepburn, and Richard S.J. Tol. 2011. "Checking the Price Tag on Catastrophe: The Social Cost of Carbon under Non-Linear Climate Response." *ESRI Working Paper* 392.

Clarke, Leon, Jae Edmonds, Volker Krey, Richard Richels, Steven Rose, and Massimo Tavoni. 2009. "International Climate Policy Architectures: Overview of the EMF 22 International Scenarios." *Energy Economics* 31, supplement 2: S64-S81.

Council of Economic Advisers. 2014. *Economic Report of the President, 2014.*

Dasgupta, Partha. 2008. "Discounting Climate Change." *Journal of Risk and Uncertainty* 37, 2/3: 141-169.

Dell, Melissa, Benjamin F. Jones, Benjamin A. Olken. 2013. "What Do We Learn from the Weather? The New Climate-Economy Literature." *Journal of Economic Literature*, forthcoming.

Deschênes, Olivier and Michael Greenstone. 2011. "Climate Change, Mortality, and Adaptation: Evidence from Annual Fluctuations in Weather in the US." *American Economic Journal: Applied Economics* 3, 4: 152-185.

Dietz, Simon. 2011. "High Impact, Low Probability? An Empirical Analysis of Risk in the Economics of Climate Change." *Climatic Change* 108, 3: 519-541.

Edmonds, Jae, Leon Clarke, John Lurz, and J. Macgregor Wise. 2008. "Stabilizing CO_2 Concentrations with Incomplete International Cooperation." *Climate Policy* 8, 4: 355-376.

Graff Zivin, Joshua and Matthew Neidell. 2014. "Temperature and the Allocation of Time: Implications for Climate Change." *Journal of Labor Economics* 32, 1: 1-26.

Gurney, Andrew, Helal Ahammad, and Melanie Ford. 2009. "The Economics of Greenhouse Gas Mitigation: Insights from Illustrative Global Abatement Scenarios Modelling." *Energy Economics* 31, supplement 2: S174-S186.

Hwang, In Chang, Richard S.J. Tol, and Marjan W. Hofkes. 2013. "Tail-Effect and the Role of Greenhouse Gas Emissions Control." *University of Sussex Working Paper* Series 6613.

Intergovernmental Panel on Climate Change, Working Group I contribution to the Fifth Assessment Report (IPCC WG I AR5). 2013. *Climate Change 2013: The Physical Science Basis*.

Intergovernmental Panel on Climate Change, Working Group II contribution to the Fifth Assessment Report (IPCC WG II AR5). 2014. *Climate Change 2014: Impacts, Adaptation and Vulnerability*.

Intergovernmental Panel on Climate Change, Working Group III contribution to the Fifth Assessment Report (IPCC WG III AR5). 2014. *Climate Change 2014: Mitigation of Climate Change*.

Jaffe, Adam and Karen Palmer. 1997. "Environmental Regulation and Innovation: A Panel Data Study." *Review of Economics and Statistics* 79, 4: 610-619.

Jakob, Michael, Gunnar Luderer, Jan Steckel, Massimo Tavoni, and Stephanie Monjon. 2012. "Time to Act Now? Assessing the Costs of Delaying Climate Measures and Benefits of Early Action." *Climatic Change* 114, 1: 79-99.

Joughin, Ian, Benjamin E. Smith, and Brooke Medley. 2014. "Marine Ice Sheet Collapse Potentially Underway for the Thwaites Glacier Basin, West Antarctica." *Science* 344, 6185: 735-738.

Kopits, Elizabeth, Alex Marten, and Ann Wolverton. 2013. "Incorporating 'Catastrophic' Climate Change into Policy Analysis." *Climate Policy* ahead-of-print: 1-28.

Krey, Volker and Keywan Riahi. 2009. "Implications of Delayed Participation and Technology Failure for the Feasibility, Costs, and Likelihood of Staying Below Temperature Targets— Greenhouse Gas Mitigation Scenarios for the 21st Century." *Energy Economics* 31, supplement 2: S94-S106.

Lanjouw, Jean and Ashoka Mody. 1996. "Innovation and the International Diffusion of Environmentally Responsive Technology." *Research Policy* 25, 4: 549-571.

Lemoine, Derek and Christian Traeger. 2012. "Tipping Points and Ambiguity in the Economics of Climate Change." *NBER Working Paper* 18230.

Link, P. Michael and Richard S.J. Tol. 2011. "Estimation of the Economic Impact of Temperature Changes Induced by a Shutdown of the Thermohaline Circulation: An Application of FUND." *Climactic Change* 104, 2: 287-304.

Litterman, Bob. 2013. "What is the Right Price for Carbon Emissions?" *Regulation* 36, 2: 38-51.

Loulou, Richard, Maryse Labriet, and Amit Kanudia. 2009. "Deterministic and Stochastic Analysis of Alternative Climate Targets under Differentiated Cooperation Regimes." *Energy Economics* 31, supplement 2: S131-S143.

Luderer, Gunnar, Valentina Bosetti, Michael Jakob, Marian Leimbach, Jan Steckel, Henri Waisman, and Ottmar Edenhofer. 2012. "The Economics of Decarbonizing the Energy System – Results and Insights from the RECIPE Model Intercomparison." *Climatic Change* 114, 1: 9-37.

Luderer, Gunnar, Robert C. Pietzcker, Christoph Bertram, Elmar Kriegler, Malte Meinshausen, and Ottmar Edenhofer. 2013. "Economic Mitigation Challenges: How Further Delay Closes the Door for Achieving Climate Targets." *Environmental Research Letters* 8, 3.

McKibbin, Warwick J., Adele C. Morris, and Peter J. Wilcoxen. 2014. "The Economic Consequences of Delay in U.S. Climate Policy." Brookings: The Climate and Energy Economics Project.

Millner, Antony. 2013. "On Welfare Frameworks and Catastrophic Climate Risks." *Journal of Environmental Economics and Management* 65, 2: 310-325.

National Research Council. 2010. *Limiting the Magnitude of Future Climate Change*. Washington, D.C.: The National Academies Press

National Research Council. 2011. *Climate Stabilization Targets: Emissions, Concentrations, and Impacts over Decades to Millennia*. Washington D.C.: The National Academies Press.

National Research Council. 2013. *Abrupt Impacts of Climate Change: Anticipating Surprises*. Washington D.C.: The National Academies Press.

Newbold, Stephen and Adam Daigneault. 2009. "Climate Response Uncertainty and the Benefits of Greenhouse Gas Emissions Reductions." *Environmental and Resource Economics* 44, 3: 351-377.

Nordhaus, William D. 2008. *A Question of Balance: Weighing the Options on Global Warming Policies*. New Haven: Yale University Press.

Nordhaus, William D. 2011. "The Economics of Tail Events with an Application to Climate Change." *Review of Environmental Economics and Policy* 5, 2: 240-257.

Nordhaus, William D. 2012. "Economic Policy in the Face of Severe Tail Events." *Journal of Public Economic Theory* 14, 2: 197-219.

Nordhaus, William D. 2013. *The Climate Casino: Risk, Uncertainty, and Economics for a Warming World*. New Haven: Yale University Press.

Pindyck, Robert S. 2011. "Fat Tails, Thin Tails, and Climate Change Policy." *Review of Environmental Economics and Policy* 5, 2: 258-274.

Pindyck, Robert S. 2012. "Uncertain Outcomes and Climate Change Policy." *Journal of Environmental Economics and Management* 63, 3: 289-303.

Pindyck, Robert S. 2013. "Climate Change Policy: What do the Models tell us?" *Journal of Economic Literature* 51, 3: 860-872.

Popp, David. 2003. "Pollution Control Innovations and the Clean Air Act of 1990." *Journal of Policy Analysis and Management* 22, 4: 641-660.

Popp, David. 2006. "International Innovation and Diffusion of Air Pollution Control Technologies: The effects of NO_X and SO_2 Regulation in the U.S., Japan, and Germany." *Journal of Environmental Economics and Management* 51, 1: 46-71.

Popp, David, Richard G. Newell, and Adam B. Jaffe. 2010. "Energy, the Environment, and Technological Change." In *Handbook of the Economics of Innovation* 2: 873-937.

Pycroft, Jonathan, Lucia Vergano, Chris Hope, Daniele Paci, and Juano Carlos Ciscar. 2011. "A Tale of Tails: Uncertainty and the Social Cost of Carbon Dioxide." *Economics* 5, 22: 1-29.

Riahi, Keywan, Elmar Kriegler, Nils Johnson, Christoph Bertram, Michel den Elzen, Jiyong Eom, Michiel Schaeffer, Jae Edmonds, Morna Isaac, Volker Krey, Thomas Longden, Gunnar Luderer, Aurélie Méjean, David L. McCollum, Silvana Mimai, Hal Turton, Detlef P. van Vuuren, Kenichi Wada, Valentina Bosetti, Pantelis Caprosm, Patrick Criqui, Meriem Hamdi-Cherif, Mikiko Kainuma, and Ottmar Edenhofer. 2014. "Locked into Copenhagen Pledges—Implications of Short-Term Emission Targets for the Cost and Feasibility of Long-Term Climate Goals." *Technological Forecasting and Social Change*. In Press.

Richels, Richard G., Thomas F. Rutherford, Geoffrey J. Blanford, and Leon Clarke. 2007. "Managing the Transition to Climate Stabilization." *Climatic Policy* 7, 5: 409-428.

Rignot, Eric, Jeremie Mouginot, Mathieu Morlighem, Helene Seroussi, and Bernd Scheuchl. 2014. "Widespread, Rapid Grounding Line Retreat of Pine Island, Thwaites, Smith, and Kohler Glaciers, West Antarctica, from 1992 to 2011." *Geophysical Research Letters* 41, 10: 3502-3509.

Roe, Gerard H. and Yoram Bauman. 2013. "Climate Sensitivity: Should the Climate Tail Wag the Policy Dog?" *Climatic Change* 117, 4: 647-662.

Russ, Peter and Tom van Ierland. 2009. "Insights on Different Participation Schemes to Meet Climate Goals." *Energy Economics* 31, supplement 2: S163-S173.

Tol, Richard S.J. 2009. "The Feasibility of Low Concentration Targets: An Application of FUND." *Energy Economics* 31, supplement 2: S121-S130.

Tol, Richard S.J. 2014. "Correction and Update: The Economic Effects of Climate Change." *Journal of Economic Perspectives* 28, 2: 221-226.

United States Environmental Protection Agency. 2014. "Carbon Pollution Emission Guidelines for Existing Stationary Sources: Electric Utility Generating Units." https://www.federalregister.gov/articles/2014/06/18/2014-13726/carbon-pollution-emission-guidelines-for-existing-stationary-sources-electric-utility-generating

(USGCRP) U.S. Global Change Research Program. 2014. *Climate Change Impacts in the United States: The Third National Climate Assessment.*

van der Ploeg, Frederick. 2014. "Abrupt Positive Feedback and the Social Cost of Carbon." *European Economic Review* 67: 28-41.

van der Ploeg, Frederick and Aart de Zeeuw. 2013. "Climate Policy and Catastrophic Change: Be Prepared and Avert Risk." *OxCarre Working Papers* 118, Oxford Centre for the Analysis of Resource Rich Economies, University of Oxford.

van Vliet, Jasper, Michael G.J. den Elzen, and Detlef P. van Vuuren. 2009. "Meeting Radiative Forcing Targets under Delayed Participation." *Energy Economics* 31, supplement 2: S152-S162.

Waldhoff, Stephanie A. and Allen A. Fawcett. 2011. "Can Developed Economies Combat Dangerous Anthropogenic Climate Change Without Near-Term Reductions from Developing Economies?" *Climatic Change* 107, 3/4: 635–641.

Waldhoff, Stephanie, Jeremy Martinich, Marcus Sarofim, Ben DeAngelo, James McFarland, Lesley Jantarasami, Kate Shouse, Allison Crimmins, Sara Ohrel, and Jia Li. 2014. "Overview of the Special Issue: A multi-model framework to achieve consistent evaluation of climate change impacts in the United States." *Climatic Change*, forthcoming.

Weitzman, Martin. 2009. "On Modeling and Interpreting the Economics of Catastrophic Climate Change." *The Review of Economics and Statistics* 91, 1: 1-19.

Weitzman, Martin. 2011. "Fat-Tailed Uncertainty in the Economics of Catastrophic Climate Change." *Review of Environmental Issues and Policy* 5, 2: 275-292.

Weitzman, Martin. 2012. "GHG Targets as Insurance against Catastrophic Climate Damages." *Journal of Public Economic Theory* 14, 2: 221-244.

Weitzman, Martin. 2013. "Tail-Hedge Discounting and the Social Cost of Carbon." *Journal of Economic Literature* 51, 3: 873-882.

Weitzman, Martin. 2014. "Fat Tails and the Social Cost of Carbon*." American Economic Review: Papers & Proceedings* 104, 5: 544-546.

Appendix: Literature on Delay Costs

This appendix lists the studies reviewed Section II and used in the meta-analysis, and briefly describes the scenarios they analyzed.

The EMF22 project engaged ten leading integrated assessment models to analyze the climate and economic consequences of delay scenarios. The EMF22 studies consist of Loulou, Labriet, and Kanudia (2009), Tol (2009), Gurney, Ahammad, and Ford (2009), van Vliet, den Elzen, and van Vuuren (2009), Blanford, Richels, and Rutherford (2009), Krey and Riahi (2009), Calvin et al. (2009a, 2009b), Russ and van Ierland (2009), and Bosetti, Carraro, and Tavoni (2009), with Clarke et al. (2009) providing an overview of the project.[28] Among other objectives, each study estimates the mitigation costs associated with five climate targets under both an immediate action scenario and a harmonized delay scenario. The targets are 450, 550, and 650 ppm CO_2e in 2100, and the models consider the first two targets alternatively allowing or prohibiting an overshoot before 2100.[29] In the delay scenario, only more developed countries (minus Russia) begin mitigation immediately in 2012 in a coordinated fashion (i.e., with the same carbon pricing), with some countries delaying action until 2030, and remaining countries delay action until 2050. These scenarios enable calculating the additional mitigation costs associated with delay for each concentration target.

The AMPERE project engaged nine modeling teams to analyze the climate and economic consequences of global emissions following the proposed policy stringency of the national pledges from the Copenhagen Accord and Cancún Agreements to 2030. (The AMPERE scenarios were not included in the meta-analysis in Section II because Riahi et al. (2014) did not provide sufficient information to calculate the percent increase in mitigation costs for each delay scenario.) One of the questions addressed by this project is the economic costs of delaying policies to reach CO2e concentration targets of 450 and 550 ppm in 2100 (Riahi et al. 2014). Eight models simulate pairs of policy scenarios reaching each target. One simulation in each pair assumes that all countries act immediately in a coordinated fashion (i.e., with the same carbon pricing), while the other simulation assumes that all countries follow the less stringent emissions commitments made during the Copenhagen Accord and Cancun Agreements until 2030, when coordinated international action begins.

The meta-analysis includes the following studies not associated with either AMPERE or EMF22: Jakob et al. (2012); Luderer et al. (2012, 2013); Edmonds et al. (2008); Richels et al. (2007), and Bosetti et al. (2009). Jakob et al. (2012) consider a 10-year delay of mitigation efforts to reach a 450 ppm CO_2 target by 2100, including variations where more developed countries implement mitigation immediately. Luderer et al. (2012) consider a similar 10-year delay and the same 450 ppm CO_2 target by 2100, with a scenario where Europe and all other industrialized countries

---

[28] Russ and van Ierland (2009) did not present estimates of total delay costs, so this paper is not included in the meta-analysis in Section II.

[29] We included three additional scenarios in van Vliet, den Elzen, and van Vuuren (2009) with alternate targets and models that were not reported in Clarke et al. (2009).

begin mitigation efforts in 2010. Luderer et al. (2013) analyze a scenario where countries implement fragmented policies before coordinating efforts in 2015, 2020, or 2030 to meet a target of 2°C above preindustrial levels by 2100, allowing for overshooting. Edmonds et al. (2008) consider targets of 450, 550, and 660 ppm CO_2, with newly developed and developing countries delaying climate action from a start date of 2012 to 2020, 2035 and 2050. Richels et al. (2007) estimate the additional cost of delay by newly developing countries until 2050 for a 450 and 550 ppm CO_2 target. Finally, Bosetti et al. (2009) estimate the additional cost when all countries delay climate action for 20 years with a goal of reaching a 550 ppm and 650 ppm CO_2e target by 2100.

www.ingramcontent.com/pod-product-compliance
Lightning Source LLC
Chambersburg PA
CBHW060808290526

45792CB00005BA/1564